The Sound Snatcher
How The Vacuum Cleaner Got Its Noise.

Written by
Linda Bryan Sabin

Illustrations by
Valerie Bouthyette

First Edition: Copyright © Linda Bryan Sabin, 2009
Illustrations Copyright © Valerie Bouthyette, 2009

All rights reserved. No part of this book may be reproduced without written permission from the publisher. Illustrations may not be used for products or any other media without written permission from the publisher and the illustrator.

Printed in the United States of America in North Mankato, Minnesota
082709
1-0809

All books published by L & M Partners, Peeking Kitty Books are manufactured with PCW recycled paper and vegetable or soy based ink.

First published 2009 by L & M Partners
and Peeking Kitty Books
peekingkitty.com
P.O. Box 2711, Sunnyvale, California 94087-4545

ISBN 978-0-9841633-0-4 (library binding)
Library of Congress Catalog Card Number 2009-90-7871
Library of Congress Cataloging-in-Publication Data
The Sound Snatcher, How the Vacuum Cleaner Got Its Noise
By Bryan Sabin, Linda; Illustrations by V. Bouthyette. p.cm. – (Word fun)
Summary: Rhyme, the sounds in the household the vacuum cleaner "eats", interactive questions (1. Sounds Fiction. 2. Stories in rhyme)

Dedication

For my Dad, who taught me to think and always told me I could do anything I put my mind to, and for my Mom, who gave me the heart, the spirit and the faith to try.

What's in the closet and down the long hall?

It's the Sound Snatcher waiting for hunger to call. Someone lets him out, plugs him in, gives him power. The Sound Snatcher's looking for sounds to devour. So…

Whizzing and wheezing with a sound
quite displeasing, he wiggles and waggles his way.
His green hose-of-a-nose and four fast wheeling
toes come sniffling and snuffling for prey.

He was made to eat dirt but some sound bites can't hurt so along with dust and the fluffle, he sucks in the sound he finds lying around. Each sweet taste for him like a truffle.

That clock on the wall? Not tick "talking" at all when the Sound Snatcher snuffles its tick.
He picks up the sound of feet walking around never missing a step with his lick.

Even the rain…a sound usually quite plain…
is reduced to silent plip plops.

And your conversation? It's just reverberation,
now lost in The Sound Snatcher's chops.

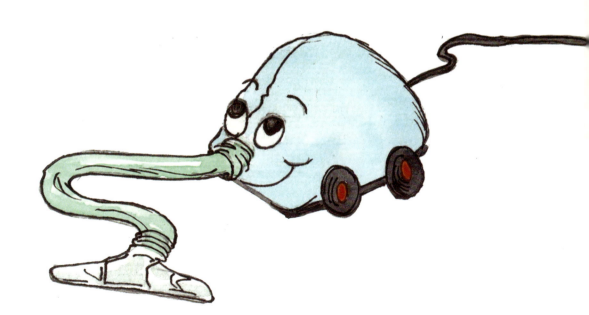

There is sound in his nose
    so the faster he goes...
        and you think his bag belly will pop.

His roar just grows louder with each bite of sound chowder! Oh when will his sound snatching stop?

The TV ball game? ...it just isn't the same when he snatches the cheers and announcing.

The crack of the bat? ...he even snatched that and the sound of that basketball bouncing.

The bacon that sizzles? The faucet that drizzles? The tea kettle's whistle? They're gone.
He snatched without wincing the dishwasher's rinsing. How long can this snatching go on?

No sounds can out loud him…

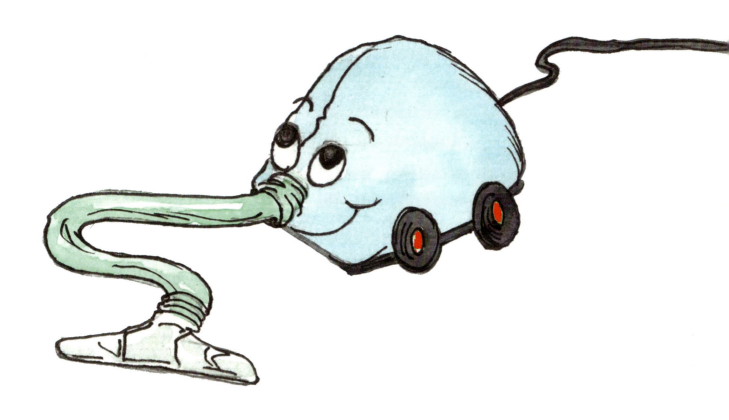

no ear muff can shroud him, as The Snatcher continues his prowling…

The cat's purr and meow?
    They are both missing now
        and so is your faithful dog's howling.

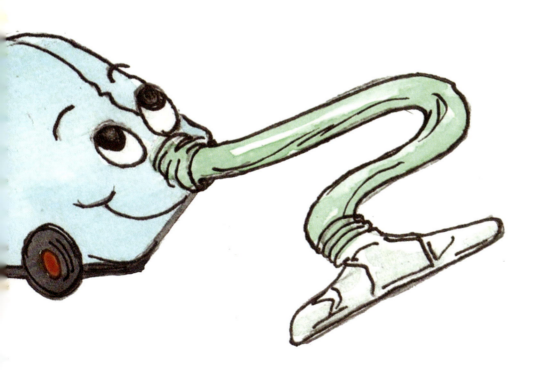

He skwurgles and gurgles
       with low thrashing swirgles,
as he crosses the floors with delight.

Each room he explores
       through the hallways and doors,
gobbling all sound in sight.

He inhales the laughter he saved for dessert,
so pleased with his tasty sound feast...

He grins as he groans
          down to low moaning tones…
this horrible sound snatching beast.

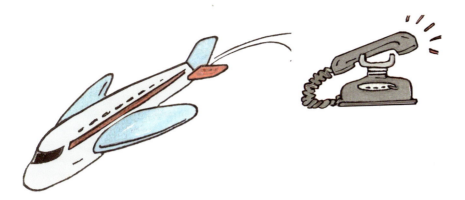

There are no more sound crumbs… so The Snatcher's roar hums. There are no more sounds left for his diet.

He sound-snatched them all, every sound large and small. And the only sound left now is…

LET'S TALK ABOUT THE BOOK

Let's Talk About the Book

1. Do you have a Sound Snatcher at your house? Where do you keep it? *(Answers vary)*

2. What do most people call the Sound Snatcher? *(A vacuum cleaner)*

3. Are you frightened by the vacuum? Why? Why not? *(Answers vary)*

4. Where was The Sound Snatcher at the beginning of the story and at the end of the story? *(The closet down the long hall, sleeping, unplugged)*

5. What was the first sound The Sound Snatcher snatched? *(The clock)* How many of the other sounds can you remember? *(Answers vary)*

6. What character, besides The Sound Snatcher, appears on every page? *(Kitty)* Go back through the book and find him.

7. Why are the fish, the sock, the man in the picture and the plant smiling when The Sound Snatcher is in the room? (*These things do not make any sound so they are not afraid of being "snatched."*)

   Look through the book and find these and other quiet things.

8. Look through the book and find: the boys name, the dog's name, the cat's name, Grandma's name? Hint: The kitty's favorite color is yellow the dog's favorite color is red. (*Mark, Mira, Pooter, Grandma Kay*)

9. What is your favorite sound in the book, in your house, in the world? Why? What is your least favorite sound in the book, in the house, in the world? Why? *(Answers vary)*

10. Can you name other loud things that "snatch sounds" Hint: find the page with the ear muffs to get ideas about things that make loud sounds.

The Words I Heard

Vocabulary

The Power of Words

Words are very important and very powerful. People can learn a lot about who you are by what you say and how you say it. When you want to say exactly the right thing, the more words you know, the more choices you have. This is called vocabulary.(Noun, pronounced vo kab u lar E) It means all the words understood and used by a person. Your vocabulary grows as you grow.

There are probably some words in this book that you did not know. Now you can learn them and use them whenever you choose. On the next pages you will find new words you may want to learn.

The Words I Heard (My New Vocabulary)

blaring verb – (bl air ing) to sound loudly and harshly

chowder noun – (chau der) a thick soup often made with clams, fish, corn, potatoes and milk

conversation – noun (kan-vEr-sA-shEn) to talk, to share by speaking ideas, opinions and feelings

devour – verb (dEh-vaur) to eat or swallow, to eat greedily (as if you won't get anymore and you want all the food for yourself)

displeasing – verb (dis plEz ing) something that does not make you happy; to displease, to annoy, dissatisfy, or disappoint

drizzles – verb (driz-zels) from noun drizzle, a light rain or a tiny drip, small leak or trickle

explore – verb (ik splor) to go and find, to search, investigate; often for something new

gobbling – verb (gah- bel- ing) to eat fast, greedy, and sometimes in a noisy way.

groans – verb (gr-oh-n) a low-pitched, long drawn out sound associated with pain or dislike

gurgles – verb (gur girls), to make a noise like a bubbling flow of liquid

horrible – adjective (hor ih bel) not nice, very bad or ugly; often causing one to be fearful

inhales – verb (ihn-hels) to breath in; to take in by breathing

moaning – verb (mone- ing) a long, low, sad cry

parakeet – noun (paer a kEt) a small parrot (bird)

prey – noun (prA), something that is being hunted; usually to be eaten

prowling – verb (proul ing) to move around slowly, secretly; roaming quietly in search of something

reduced – verb (rE dusd) to make less in amount or size

reverberation – noun (rih vuhr ber A shen) the continuing on of a sound after the sources has been cut off; an echo

shroud – noun (sh raud) a wrap or blanket that covers, hides or covers up

snatch/snatching/snatches – verb (sna ch) to grab quickly. Noun (snatcher) someone or something that grabs things quickly

snuffles, snuffling – verb (snuh- fel) to breathe or speak in a noisy way with whine; to cover up, put out, snuff out

thrashing – verb (thra sh ing) to move around in a wild, whipping, uncontrollable way

truffle – noun (truh-fel) a bite sized piece of very rich chocolate candy and also a type of wild mushroom (fungi); both considered a very special treat or delicacy

usually – noun (yu zhu lE) from usual which means common place, most of the time, ordinary

wheezing – verb (wiz-ing) to breath with a hoarse whistling sound

wincing – verb (win-ss-ing) to pull suddenly back or away from something painful or frightening

More Word Fun

The way words rhyme (sound alike) and the way they sound when spoken or used in a sentence makes learning, reading and writing fun. It is always best to learn and use real words, but sometimes when you cannot find or do not know a real word for what you want to say, it is fun to use your imagination and make up your "very own words".

Here is a list of the author's "very own words":

fluffle – noun (flah fel) a soft, down like, feathery substance; a combination of dust, pet fur, thread etc. (sometimes called dust bunnies)

squwurgles – verb (skwir gils) a word made by putting the words squirm and gurgle together
    squirm – noun (sk worm) to wiggle
    gurgle – (see gurgling above)

swirgles – noun (swir- gils) a word made by putting the words swirl and gurgle together
    swirl – to move along in a twirling, spinning motion
    gurgle – (see gurgles above)